AWS PrivateLink Traffic Flow Troubleshooting

Table of Contents

Chapter 1. Introduction

In this Special Report, we delve into the increasingly pertinent topic of "AWS PrivateLink Traffic Flow Troubleshooting." Designed for both technical experts and novices alike, this report provides an essential, understandable blueprint for successfully navigating through complex scenarios inherent in AWS PrivateLink operations. A deeper look into this robust service that securely exposes services across AWS accounts can prove daunting due to technical intricacies. However, there's no need to fear—this report simplifies the densest technical concepts, making it an indispensable tool in your AWS problem-solving arsenal. Whether you're wrangling with connectivity issues, latency hitches, or private DNS challenges, this easy-to-follow guide will help you troubleshoot effectively and efficiently. Don't get lost in the technical maze, let our special report illuminate your path to successful AWS PrivateLink Traffic Flow Troubleshooting.

Chapter 2. Understanding AWS PrivateLink: Basics and Beyond

AWS PrivateLink is a distinctly designed service that provides secure access to services hosted on AWS. Acting as a conduit, it simplifies and secures connectivity between VPCs (Virtual Private Clouds), AWS services, and on-premises applications.

2.1. What is AWS PrivateLink?

Amazon Web Services (AWS) PrivateLink is a networking service that allows for the secure access of services across various accounts and Virtual Private Clouds (VPCs). Traditional access protocols expose data to the public internet, making it vulnerable to security breaches. PrivateLink helps mitigate this problem by providing private connectivity between VPCs, AWS services, and on-premises applications, without exposing the data traffic to the public internet.

2.2. Key Concepts of AWS PrivateLink

Understanding the following key concepts of AWS PrivateLink will provide a solid foundation for troubleshooting connectivity issues, latency problems, and private DNS challenges:

1. **Service Endpoints:** These are the entry points for traffic destined to an AWS service or a VPC endpoint service privately powered by AWS PrivateLink. Service endpoints exist within the consumer VPC.

2. **Endpoint Services:** These are an AWS PrivateLink-powered service that consumers can access over an interface VPC endpoint.

3. Service Providers and Service Consumers: A service provider owns and manages an endpoint service. A service consumer uses an interface VPC endpoint to connect with the endpoint service via PrivateLink.

4. Network Load Balancers: This feature distributes incoming traffic across multiple targets within an endpoint service. The network load balancer ensures that the processing load is evenly distributed among these targets to ensure optimal performance.

2.3. Benefits of Employing AWS PrivateLink

AWS PrivateLink offers several benefits to users that are worth understanding to gain a comprehensive view of the service:

1. Enhanced Security: PrivateLink secures applications and data, minimizing exposure to threats by avoiding the public internet for data traffic between VPCs, AWS services, and on-site applications.

2. Easy Scalability: PrivateLink enables you to connect applications across different accounts and VPCs, providing an efficient scalability solution.

3. Simplified Network Architecture: By using AWS PrivateLink, you can significantly simplify your network architecture. It eliminates the need for an Internet Gateway, NAT devices, VPN connections, or AWS Direct Connect for intercommunication between resources.

4. Reduced Data Transfer Costs: Data transferred between VPCs and services do not traverse the public internet or leave the AWS network. Therefore, it reduces the overall data transfer charges.

2.4. How Does AWS PrivateLink Work?

AWS PrivateLink provides a way for VPCs to privately connect to AWS services without requiring access over the public internet, VPN, or AWS Direct Connect. It does so by creating private connections between VPCs and services. These private connections are established via VPC endpoint services powered by PrivateLink and are accessible via VPC endpoint interfaces in the client VPC.

These private connections remain within the Amazon network, providing more secure access compared to traditional methods which often require data transmission over the public internet.

2.5. Common Use Cases for AWS PrivateLink

The unique capabilities of AWS PrivateLink have led to its application across a range of use cases:

1. Multi-account AWS Environments: AWS PrivateLink is often employed in environments where multiple AWS accounts exist. Its robust capability to handle connections across VPCs makes it a favored choice.

2. Third-party SaaS Solutions: For enterprises using third-party SaaS solutions that are hosted on AWS, PrivateLink can offer private connectivity from their VPC to these SaaS applications.

3. Data Sovereignty and Compliance: PrivateLink supports compliance with specific regulations by ensuring that traffic between resources does not traverse the internet, keeping your data within a prescriptive geographical boundary.

4. Service Centralization: For enterprises utilizing AWS organizations, specific shared services can be centralized using AWS PrivateLink.

In the next section, we'll delve deeper into these use cases and explore how to troubleshoot potential issues related to them.

2.6. Tying it All Together: AWS PrivateLink Architecture

AWS PrivateLink utilizes a specific component, namely the Interface VPC endpoint (powered by ENIs) that remains within the consumer's VPC. The endpoint provides reliable and secure communication with services across the AWS ecosystem without traversing the public internet.

This setup is essential because it provides a seamless way to access services across AWS accounts, AWS services, and on-premise applications. It significantly simplifies the network architecture by eliminating the need for internet gateways, VPNs, AWS Direct Connect, or NAT devices to communicate.

Importantly, by utilizing AWS PrivateLink, data is secured against a broad range of security threats. All communications between the services and the consumer's VPC occur over the Amazon network, fundamentally reducing the risk of data exposure to threats.

The layer of protection AWS PrivateLink provides is absolutely essential for businesses striving to gain a balance between necessary flexibility and robust security in an increasingly complex digital world. Utilize this guide to help you navigate through AWS PrivateLink's technical intricacies – it's the helping hand you need to troubleshoot effectively and navigate the sometimes daunting world of AWS operations. By doing so, you are taking an essential step towards securing your business in the digital age.

Chapter 3. Establishing Connections with PrivateLink

No matter the scale of your operations on AWS, establishing firm connections between your services through PrivateLink is vital. This process, while being crucial for the smooth function of your applications, requires an acute understanding of the underlying principles and intricacies involved. In this section, we will walk step-by-step through the processes of establishing connections via PrivateLink, delve into some of the most common difficulties you may encounter, and offer effective troubleshooting strategies for such situations.

Chapter 4. Setting the Course: Understanding AWS PrivateLink Communication Flow

Before looking at how to establish connections, it is essential that we understand how traffic flows within AWS PrivateLink. The primary purpose of AWS PrivateLink is to allow private connectivity between AWS services and your VPC, leveraging a network link instead of exposing your traffic through the public internet. In other words, PrivateLink provides an anchor to ensure traffic stays within the AWS network.

This service also allows access to services across AWS accounts and VPCs, enabling you to isolate your instances for enhanced security while reducing the data transfer costs. This is achieved by creating endpoint services and endpoints in your VPCs. Traffic enters and leaves your VPC through these points, devoid of going through the public internet.

Chapter 5. Preparing the Infrastructure: Prerequisites for Connection Establishment

Before establishing connections, ensure you have the following prerequisites completed:

- An AWS account: You will need an AWS account to create and manage the necessary resources to establish a connection.

- An established VPC: A Virtual Private Cloud (VPC) is where the private link endpoints will be set up.

- CIDR blocks: For your VPCs to connect over PrivateLink, they must not have overlapping CIDR blocks.

- Necessary IAM permissions: Make sure you have the necessary Identity and Access Management (IAM) permissions to create and manage PrivateLink connections.

Chapter 6. Sailing Ahead: Establishing AWS PrivateLink Connections

1. Start by creating a Network Load Balancer (NLB) in your provider VPC. The NLB should be designed to route traffic from your consumer VPC to different resources in your provider VPC. Remember, your NLB will not show up in the AWS Management Console of your consumer VPC.

2. Next, create an endpoint service in the provider VPC. You will need to associate the created NLB with this service.

3. Move to your consumer's AWS Management Console and create a VPC endpoint for the service you created above. Make sure this endpoint is within the same region to avoid latency issues.

4. In your provider VPC's console, approve the connection request from your consumer VPC. After this, the status of your VPC endpoint service should change to 'Available,' signifying that VPC endpoint and VPC endpoint service are now connected.

Chapter 7. Anticipating Rough Waters: Common Challenges and Their Solutions

Establishing connections with PrivateLink is not without its hurdles. Given below are some common challenges users encounter, along with possible solutions:

1. **No connection between VPCs**: Firstly, verify that both your VPCs are correctly set up without overlapping CIDR blocks. Ensure that the necessary IAM permissions to create connections are in place.

2. **VPC endpoint status remains 'Pending'**: If the VPC endpoint status remains 'Pending' after a connection request, it could indicate that the provider has not approved your request. Ensure the provider approves the connection request on their end.

3. **Unable to access the service**: Ensure your service permissions and security groups in your consumer and provider VPCs allow inbound and outbound traffic.

Remember, establishing connections with AWS PrivateLink is a layered process. Whether you're an expert or a beginner, understanding each step—its implications and possible pitfalls—is critical for running smooth operations in AWS. With the necessary know-how and cautious foresight, you will be able to navigate the powerful tool that is AWS PrivateLink with ease and confidence.

Chapter 8. Securing and Monitoring Traffic Flow

Securing and monitoring traffic flow with AWS PrivateLink involves a multi-faceted approach. This consists of implementing security measures, setting up health checks, and using various AWS services and features to monitor traffic.

8.1. Implementing Security Measures

When setting up your PrivateLink connection, the first primary concerns should be initiating proper security measures to ensure the safety of your data transfer.

Network-level Isolation

With AWS PrivateLink, your services become accessible on your own private network, isolating them from public networks to reduce opportunities for attackers. Additionally, you can use an Amazon-provided IP address or bring your own to guarantee better network-level isolation.

Security Groups and Network Access Control Lists (ACLs)

You should apply security groups to endpoints, and these security groups act as a virtual firewall for your endpoint. Network ACLs operate at the subnet level and should be implemented as another measure of protection. They act as a second layer of security and can defend against potential attacks even if your security groups fail.

Amazon VPC Traffic Mirroring

VPC Traffic Mirroring duplicates inbound and outbound traffic at the Elastic Network Interface (ENI) level and sends it to out-of-band security and monitoring appliances, which allows in-depth packet-level inspection. This can be utilized in PrivateLink to ensure no unwanted traffic sneaks through, further solidifying security and data protection.

8.2. Setting Up Health Checks

Continuous health checks are critical to the effective functioning of your AWS PrivateLink and need to be set up correctly for optimal results.

AWS Route 53 Health Checks

Route 53 health checks can be utilized to verify the health of your endpoints and determine if they require maintenance or repair. Route 53 health checks monitor the health of your resources, such as web servers and email servers, by reaching out to your endpoint and awaiting a response. If there isn't a response, Route 53 will classify the endpoint as unhealthy.

AWS CloudWatch

CloudWatch can be used to collect and track metrics, which can provide useful data on the health of your PrivateLink. You can create alarms that send notifications or automatically make changes to resources based on rules defined in AWS CloudWatch.

8.3. Monitoring Traffic with AWS Services

AWS offers a host of services to ensure robust and comprehensive traffic monitoring on your PrivateLink connection.

AWS CloudTrail

CloudTrail records AWS API calls for your account, including API calls made via the AWS Management Console, AWS SDKs, and

Command-line tools. These recorded logs can provide valuable insight by detailing who is making API requests, from which IP address, and at what time. This can assist in auditing and reviewing activity on your PrivateLink connection.

Amazon GuardDuty

GuardDuty is a threat detection service which continuously monitors to protect your AWS accounts and workloads. It uses machine learning, anomaly detection, and integrated threat intelligence to identify unauthorized behavior such as unusual API calls. This information can be vital in securing your PrivateLink connection and mitigating threats.

AWS X-Ray

X-Ray is a service that collects data about requests that your application serves and provides tools to view, filter, and gain insights into data to identify issues and opportunities for optimization. It can help in peering deeply into your application's behavior and its underlying services to manage complex and possibly multi-tiered applications.

In conclusion, securing and monitoring traffic flow with AWS PrivateLink involves several key components including implementing stringent security measures, setting up health checks, and utilizing AWS services for comprehensive traffic monitoring. By focusing on these measures and leveraging the robust AWS systems, you can greatly minimize the risk of unwanted incidents and optimize the efficiency and performance of your AWS PrivateLink.

Chapter 9. Essential Tools for Troubleshooting Issues

Before diving into the real task of troubleshooting AWS PrivateLink traffic flow, it's vital to understand the essential tools that'll aid in the process. These tools are designed to offer better visibility of your application's health and performance while helping you spot potential issues promptly—rendering them cornerstones in your troubleshooting journey.

9.1. Understanding VPC Flow Logs

Virtual Private Cloud (VPC) Flow Logs is one of the most powerful tools for troubleshooting AWS PrivateLink traffic flow issues. It records information about the IP traffic going to, and from, network interfaces in your VPC. It captures data such as source and destination IP addresses, ports, IANA protocol numbers, packet and byte counts, and allowed or denied request statuses.

To create a flow log for a VPC, subnet, or a network interface, you need to head to the Amazon VPC console, select the relevant VPC or subnet, and click on 'Create Flow Log'. You're given the choice to publish the logs to Amazon CloudWatch Logs or Amazon S3. It's worth noting that VPC Flow Logs incurs costs, particularly when stored in CloudWatch Logs.

9.2. CloudWatch Logs

AWS CloudWatch Logs service provides a platform to monitor, store, and access your log files from Amazon EC2 instances, AWS CloudTrail, and other sources. Once the VPC Flow Logs are stored on CloudWatch, you can make use of CloudWatch Log Insights to analyze the logs.

With minimal setup, Log Insights enables you to explore, analyze, and visualize your logs instantly, allowing you to troubleshoot operational issues with ease. It comes with a purpose-built query language with simple commands for fields, queries, filters, sorting, and aggregations.

9.3. Network Interfaces

Network interfaces in AWS are crucial to understanding how traffic flows through your AWS PrivateLink. A network interface is a simple networking construct that contains information about how to send or receive traffic.

Examining the settings of network interfaces can provide key insights into traffic flow. Navigate to your VPC console, choose Network Interfaces in the navigation pane, and select a particular interface for more details. For instance, look into "source/destination checks," which should typically be disabled for the network interface to send and receive traffic.

9.4. System Logs

The system logs of your resources, such as EC2 instances, are useful in diagnosing problems. They can provide insights about operations at the operating system level, perhaps identifying a misconfigured networking setting. You can view the system logs for an instance from the Amazon EC2 console.

9.5. Network Load Balancer

Network Load Balancer, integral to AWS PrivateLink, operates at the Transport Layer (Layer 4), and handles millions of requests per second. It preserves source IP, allowing the back-end applications to see the IP for incoming requests. Network Load Balancer logs can be incredibly useful in troubleshooting efforts.

You can enable logging for your Network Load Balancer on the AWS console. Once enabled, logs are sent to an S3 bucket of your choice. These logs contain information such as incoming traffic, backend resources, error codes, latency, and more.

9.6. DNS Logs

Finally, DNS logs can also be pivotal in troubleshooting AWS PrivateLink issues. AWS Route 53 or your private DNS can provide valuable information about the DNS resolution process. Tools such as `dig` and `nslookup` can disclose information about DNS resolution for a given endpoint.

9.7. Wrapping Up

All these tools are essentially part of the "AWS PrivateLink Traffic Flow Troubleshooting" toolkit. They offer the insights you need to evaluate your network performance and troubleshoot AWS PrivateLink operation issues. However, the tools are most effective when used strategically in conjunction—their combined power packs the punch for robust troubleshooting.

Understanding the integral role these tools play in troubleshooting is the first key to overcoming any potential AWS PrivateLink hurdles. As always, remember that AWS maintains an extensive documentation base for each tool mentioned, which acts as an invaluable resource in times of troubleshooting.

Chapter 10. Troubleshooting: Connectivity Concerns and Their Solutions

AWS PrivateLink is a powerful tool that bridges different AWS accounts securely, yet connectivity problems might pose severe challenges to its smooth functioning. This section explores the common connectivity troubles and potential solutions.

10.1. Identifying Common Connectivity Issues

Connectivity concerns with AWS PrivateLink can often be confusing because of the various moving components involved. Problems may originate from three primary areas:

1. Network configurations within the VPC,

2. Configuration of the AWS PrivateLink service itself,

3. DNS configurations and resolutions.

Understanding the domain in which the issue lies is the first step to addressing it effectively.

10.2. Inspecting VPC Configurations

VPC configurations form the backbone of your AWS environment. To ensure a seamless flow of traffic, you need to:

1. Check Security Groups and Network ACL rules in your VPC and confirm they allow inbound and outbound traffic for your service.

2. Verify there's an adequate route to the endpoint in your route table.

3. Make sure IP ranges do not overlap between the consumer VPC and service provider's VPC, as it can disrupt connectivity.

10.3. Understanding AWS PrivateLink Configurations

Once you've inspected VPC configurations for faults, the next step is to understand and address potential issues with AWS PrivateLink itself.

1. AWS PrivateLink Endpoint services: Each service endpoint requires correctly configured Network Load Balancer (NLB). Check to ensure that your NLB is operational and has healthy instances in each availability zone.

2. AWS PrivateLink Interface Endpoints: These endpoints allow communication with services over AWS PrivateLink. Check to verify that the endpoint you're connecting with is correctly configured in the host account and associated with an active AWS PrivateLink service.

10.4. Addressing DNS Resolutions

Problems may arise out of DNS resolution issues as well. It's crucial to:

1. See if DNS name resolution for VPC Endpoint is enabled.

2. Confirm that you are using the correct DNS hostname. AWS PrivateLink creates a unique regional DNS hostname for each endpoint.

3. In case you are using a private hosted zone in Route 53, ensure that the zone is associated with the correct VPCs.

10.5. Implementing Solutions

Once you've identified the area causing connectivity issues, the associated solution becomes clearer.

1. Network Configuration Solutions: If you identify a network-related issue, adjust the necessary controls in Security Groups and Network ACLs. If IP overlap problems exist, you might need to plan a change in your IP CIDRs to avoid this. Verify the routes in your route table.

2. PrivateLink Configuration Solutions: If issues pertain to AWS PrivateLink, correct the configurations of the endpoint services or interface endpoints. You might need to inspect your NLBs and ensure healthy instances exist in all availability zones.

3. DNS Solutions: Lastly, if the problem lies in DNS, correct your DNS settings. Make sure DNS for VPC Endpoint is enabled, the correct DNS hostname is used, and the private hosted zone is associated with the correct VPCs if you're using Route 53.

When these predefined troubleshooting steps aren't enough, AWS has another powerful tool, VPC Reachability Analyzer, which diagnoses the reachability between two resources in your VPCs. This tool could act as an additional layer of investigation for stubborn network problems.

To conclude, addressing connectivity issues with AWS PrivateLink isn't unapproachable. It involves a methodical course of identifying the problem area: either within the network configurations, AWS PrivateLink configurations, or DNS resolutions, and systematically addressing them. All the while, remember: every challenge is an opportunity to learn and enhance your understanding of your AWS environment.

Chapter 11. Decoding Latency Problems in AWS PrivateLink

Latency is a frequent adversary to smooth network operations, capable of impeding AWS PrivateLink traffic flow. As such, an effective understanding of latency, its potential causes, and the suitable remedies are indispensable. Whether you are a beginner or have a technical background, this in-depth investigation draws a comprehensive map to navigate through latency issues in AWS PrivateLink.

11.1. Recognizing Latency Symptoms

Identifying the symptoms of latency is the first step to resolving them. Typical signs include slow network responses, delayed data transfer, extended marinating time, as well as freezing or crashing applications. Further, AWS CloudWatch metrics can provide insightful data indicative of latency behaviour. Specifically:

1. Increased `NetworkPacketsOut` and `NetworkPacketsIn`: Shows the packets in transit, a rise may suggest slow packet transmission.

2. Elevated `NetworkE2ELatency`: Speaks directly to the latency between points in the network.

3. Spike in `ClientTLSNegotiationErrorCount`: Signals errors in the negotiation process, potentially due to latency.

4. Raised `NewFlowCount`: Records new flows created, a sudden increase may indicate previous flows are timing out because of latency.

11.2. Examining The Top Causes Of Latency

There are multiple potential catalysts for latency. Understanding these causes can expedite troubleshooting:

1. **Network distance**: Significant physical distances between the sender and recipient increase travel time, inducing latency.

2. **Congestion**: High traffic can strain network resources—much like a crowded highway—slowing data delivery and adding to latency.

3. **Poor-quality hardware**: Outdated or underperforming hardware can bottleneck data transfer, causing latency.

4. **Inefficient routing**: Data taking long, inefficient routes contributes to latency.

5. **Packet retransmission**: When packets are lost or faulty during transmission, retransmissions occur, imposing additional delay.

11.3. Troubleshooting Techniques and Best Practices

Effective troubleshooting involves several strategies:

1. **Network tracing tools**: Tools such as Traceroute, MTR (My traceroute) or PathPing can help identify the path packets take from source to destination.

2. **Analyzing AWS VPC Flow Logs**: The logs keep records of all IP traffic going to and from network interfaces within your VPC. Flow logs can help identify the source of increased latency.

3. **AWS CloudWatch**: Use the AWS private link metrics in CloudWatch to visualize and identify latency problems.

4. **Latency reduction software**: Software solutions can reduce latency by optimizing data routes, managing bandwidth, and prioritizing traffic.

5. **Upgrade Hardware**: Upgrading network hardware and connections can alleviate bottlenecks and reduce latency.

6. **Optimize Application Architecture**: Optimal design of your application key architectural components can to a large extent, alleviate common latency issues.

11.4. Understanding AWS PrivateLink Components

To grasp its latency problems, it is essential to understand the components of AWS PrivateLink. AWS PrivateLink consists of Network Load Balancers (NLB), Elastic Network Interfaces (ENI), and Endpoint Services. Each plays a pivotal role in managing traffic. Particular latency issues may be traceable to specific elements –

1. NLBs manage traffic between VPCs and services. Issues here may lead to latency.

2. ENIs are the point of connection for an AWS service within a VPC. If the ENI is under stress or poorly configured, latency may increase.

3. Endpoint Services are the way AWS or a custom service is made available via PrivateLink. Any problems with the configuration can result in latency.

11.5. Understanding The AWS PrivateLink Process

A detailed understanding of the journey a data packet takes via AWS PrivateLink is imperative to diagnosing latency issues. The process is as follows:

1. A client in a VPC sends a request to a service using the service's private DNS hostname.

2. Route 53 resolver rules direct the request to a Network Load Balancer (NLB) serving the Endpoint Service for the requested service within the VPC.

3. The NLB balances load by directing the traffic to one of many available Elastic Network Interfaces (ENIs).

4. Data is transferred to the service via the ENI.

5. The service processes the data and sends a response back to the client via the same route.

By thoroughly understanding network latency and its relationship with AWS PrivateLink, diagnosing and solving latency issues becomes significantly more convenient. Coupling this with effective tools and practices creates a potent problem-solving toolkit capable of alleviating common and complex latency problems. With this knowledge, you can securely and efficiently create, manage, and troubleshoot AWS PrivateLink connections.

Chapter 12. Diving into Private DNS Challenges

Let's first set the stage by understanding that AWS PrivateLink provides an additional layer of security for your VPC by creating endpoints that are solely available within your network. It proxies the traffic between the service and your VPC, ensuring that it does not traverse the public Internet. A distinguishing feature of PrivateLink is that it uses, by extension, private DNS to resolve the names of the AWS service endpoints in your VPC. However, as with any technology, complexities can arise, especially when it comes to DNS. In this chapter, we will delve into some of these challenges and offer problem-solving techniques and solutions.

12.1. The Nature of the Beast: Understanding Private DNS

To effectively troubleshoot any issue related to AWS PrivateLink, you must first have a grasp of private DNS in context. A Private DNS name is a domain name that Route 53 provides for addressing Amazon VPC instances. It's only visible to your organization and is much easier to work with than public IP addresses. The main obstacle arises when you're trying to resolve private DNS across peered VPCs or with on-premise environments via VPN or Direct Connect connection.

12.2. Resolving Private DNS Across Peered VPCs

Cross peering your VPCs can prove to be a bottleneck if not correctly set. You need to perform a series of manually executed settings to allow the resolver in one VPC to forward DNS requests to another

VPC. Duly note, on the peering connections, the DNS resolution option should be enabled, and the VPC's security groups must allow incoming traffic on UDP port 53.

12.3. Bridging the Gap with On-premise Environments

For organizations that need to use PrivateLink together with an on-premise resolver, the AWS Direct Connect or VPN connection provides a gateway for the on-premise DNS to flow seamlessly into the VPC environment. Again, security groups and network access control lists (ACLs) need to be correctly in place to allow incoming queries on the UDP and TCP port 53.

12.4. Working Around DNS Propagation Delays

Managing DNS changes in an AWS environment requires patience. It can take time for the changes to propagate across the different Amazon VPCs, which can significantly impact latency. Consider using Amazon Route 53 Resolver rules to minimize propagation times, or work around by using IP addresses directly.

12.5. Overcoming the Challenge of Limited DNS Hostnames

The number of DNS hostnames in the Amazon VPC is capped, which could limit the number of PrivateLink endpoints an enterprise can leverage. Obtain a service quota increase from AWS if you need to operate a higher number of endpoints.

12.6. Tricky Split-Horizon DNS Scenario

A typical scenario, the split-horizon DNS, where internal and external users see different DNS records for the same domain name, might be of a challenge when it comes to AWS PrivateLink. You need to create both an internal and an external DNS record for each AWS service endpoint, and configure DNS servers to forward requests for the internal domain to your Amazon VPC.

12.7. Confirming DNS Resolutions

Part of your troubleshooting process will involve confirming that your AWS Private DNS is resolving correctly. You can do this by making use of the nslookup or dig commands, and cross-checking with the expected results from the Route53 Resolver.

12.8. Navigating Private DNS with Hybrid Cloud Deployments

When dealing with hybrid-cloud deployments that include an on-premise data center and cloud environment, DNS resolution may become tricky. While it is possible to extend the Active Directory to the VPCs, AWS recommends using the Amazon Route 53 Resolver to facilitate seamless DNS resolution in a hybrid environment.

When dealing with private DNS challenges in AWS PrivateLink, keeping close tabs on your configurations, access permissions, and ensuring understanding of DNS resolution mechanisms can save you time. Remember, patience and vigilance go a long way to smooth operations in a complex environment such as this. One final takeaway would be always to keep abreast of AWS's changing landscape. Some of today's challenges may be addressed in future enhancements of the platform, and conversely, new features may pose their unique set of challenges. Staying in the learning mindset will yield dividends over the long run.

Chapter 13. Practical Case Studies in Traffic Flow Troubleshooting

The world of AWS PrivateLink Traffic Flow is filled with numerous scenarios, each presenting unique opportunities to learn and improve. Below are a few practical case studies that not only provide real-world insights but also help you develop your troubleshooting prowess.

13.1. Case Study 1: Resolving Connectivity Issues

When it comes to PrivateLink, connectivity issues are a common challenge. In a scenario where an end-user reports problems accessing a service via PrivateLink, alarm bells may start ringing. Let's delve into the troubleshooting steps following a methodical approach.

First, verify the service is accessible within the VPC.

```
[source,shell]
```

$ nc -vz private-service-vpc-endpoint 80

```
You expect output "succeeded!" If the service is
inaccessible, consider confirming the VPC endpoint
configuration.

Next, ensure the security group associated with the
```

PrivateLink endpoint permits traffic. Often,
misconfigurations in security group rules can disrupt
service accessibility. To verify this:

```shell
$ aws ec2 describe-security-groups --group-ids sg-
0abcd1234efgh5678
```

Examine the inbound and outbound rules—if they are too restrictive,
they may block traffic. Modify as necessary to allow appropriate
access.

After you've confirmed within-VPC accessibility and valid security
group rules, the next step is often to review routing tables. If there is
a conflict in your route table, AWS PrivateLink may face issues
establishing connections.

```
[source,shell]
```

```shell
$ aws ec2 describe-route-tables --route-table-id rtb-
0abcd1234efgh5678
```

Ensure the destination for your desired traffic aligns
with the correct VPC endpoint.

Lastly, test from the customer's location. If the
problem persists, the issue might stem from their
network, in which case further collaboration may be
necessary.

=== Case Study 2: Alleviating Latency Grievances

Latency is another predominant issue in AWS PrivateLink
that often roots in suboptimal route configurations.

```
Let's consider a user scenario where latency
deteriorates, affecting service performance.

Initially, evaluate current network latency using
standard tools such as 'Ping' or 'Traceroute.'
```

```
$ ping -c 5 private-service-vpc-endpoint
$ traceroute private-service-vpc-endpoint
```

Note any abnormal round-trip times (RTT) or any route that depicts significant latency.

If you notice latency issues, consider assessing your network setup—particularly subnets and availability zones (AZ). If traffic spans multiple AZs, latency might increase. Aim for a setup where the service and consumers exist in the same AZ for optimal performance.

13.2. Case Study 3: Solving Private DNS Challenges

Private DNS challenges can result from incorrect DNS settings or misconfigured Route 53 Private Hosted Zones. Consider a user scenario where DNS resolution fails for a service exposed via PrivateLink.

First, check if DNS resolution is enabled on the VPC which can be verified via the following command:

```
[source,shell]
```

$ aws ec2 describe-vpcs

```
In the output, `enableDnsSupport` and
`enableDnsHostnames` should be `true`.

Next, verify if Private DNS Name is enabled for your VPC
endpoint.
```

```
$ aws ec2 describe-vpc-endpoints --vpc-endpoint-ids
vpce-0abcd1234efgh5678
```

If it's not, enable it, and ensure there isn't any conflicting DNS namespace.

For issues persisting past these checks, delve deeper into the Route 53 Resolver rules and verify correct namespace routing.

Ultimately, these practical case studies aim to equip you with a robust strategy to approach various troubleshooting scenarios you might encounter while managing AWS PrivateLink Traffic Flow. These scenarios aren't exhaustive, but they offer a strong foundation on which you can build your mastery. With consistent practice and a methodical approach, you'll evolve from a novice problem-solver to a seasoned troubleshooter adept at navigating the twists and turns of the AWS PrivateLink labyrinth.

Chapter 14. Optimizing AWS PrivateLink for Enhanced Performance

Let's commence by understanding that optimization of AWS (Amazon Web Services) PrivateLink constitutes several facets that pivot on efficient data transfer and secure connectivity. We shall explore these concepts in detail, enabling you to apply them to your specific applications for enhanced performance.

14.1. Ingress and Egress Data Management

One crucial dimension of optimizing AWS PrivateLink is the efficient management of both incoming (ingress) and outgoing (egress) data. It's of utmost importance to consider the bandwidth and data transfer costs associated with your PrivateLink connection. Optimizing these aspects can significantly improve the performance and cost-effectiveness of your network.

Besides, you can leverage AWS CloudWatch and VPC Flow Logs to monitor your data flow, allowing you to take corrective actions. Consequently, it helps improve your network's efficiency by identifying unusual traffic patterns and bottlenecks.

14.2. Network Load Balancing

Network load balancing transparently distributes network traffic across multiple servers, ensuring no single server takes on too much load. With AWS PrivateLink, you can use Network Load Balancers (NLBs) to help distribute traffic and hence, improve network performance. This technique is particularly effective if your service end points are experiencing disproportionately high traffic.

AWS PrivateLink integrates seamlessly with NLBs. You simply need to specify the NLB while setting up the PrivateLink. At the same time, ensure the connection limit for your NLB aligns with the traffic. This method is ideal for circumventing the potential for 'hotspot' issues or overloaded connection points.

14.3. Implement AWS Direct Connect

Dedicated network connections from your premises to AWS can enhance the performance of your PrivateLink. AWS Direct Connect bypasses the public Internet, providing a more consistent network experience and reducing bandwidth costs. When configured correctly, Direct Connect accelerates data transfers to and from your VPCs, thereby enhancing the efficiency of your PrivateLink.

14.4. Network Packet Size and MTU

Network performance can suffer when there's a mismatch between the Maximum Transmission Unit (MTU) of the sender and receiver. For optimal communication over AWS PrivateLink, you must ensure both the sending and receiving entities align. Specifically, the MTU of your TCP/IP network should be set to support jumbo frames (9001 bytes). Notably, there are several ways to change MTU size, including console-based and CLI-based operations.

14.5. Endpoints and DNS

Endpoints play a considerable role in the AWS PrivateLink ecosystem. Establishing effective endpoints and configuring private DNS can enhance PrivateLink performance. Remember, communication and data transfer are mediated through endpoints using Interface VPC Endpoints and Gateway VPC Endpoints. Thus, aptly managing these key components can drastically improve the performance of your PrivateLink.

For instance, you can divide services across multiple endpoints for operational segregation. Additionally, a suitable naming scheme for endpoints and proper tagging can simplify management.

AWS also allows you to enable Private DNS, enabling simpler connections to your services. Clients can reach the service using its standard AWS DNS hostname, thereby minimizing potential connectivity issues.

14.6. Latency Optimization

If latency is a critical issue, it's recommended to position your AWS PrivateLink traffic sources and targets as close as possible. Direct connections to a nearby AWS Direct Connect location, in tandem with AWS PrivateLink, can drastically reduce latency.

Moreover, using services like Amazon CloudFront and Route 53 can help distribute your content closer to the end-users and reduce DNS lookup times, in turn, reducing latency. It's advisable to systematically evaluate and troubleshoot latency to maintain optimal performance.

14.7. Security and Compliance

Finally, while focusing on network optimization, don't overlook security and compliance. Implementing endpoint policies to control access to your services can add an extra layer of protection to your network. Regularly auditing VPC flow logs and using services like AWS Shield Advanced will help ensure your network is secure and compliant.

To sum up, optimizing AWS PrivateLink involves a blend of effective data management, network load balancing, strategic use of AWS Direct Connect, appropriate network packet size and MTU, efficient endpoint and DNS configuration, and dedicated security compliance checks.

Remember, the ultimate objective of these efforts should be to ensure seamless, secure, and fast data flow within your network. As complex as it may seem, with the right steps and tools, you can successfully optimize AWS PrivateLink for enhanced performance, managing even the most intricate of scenarios.

Chapter 15. The Future of AWS PrivateLink: Trends and Updates

As we gaze into the future, the trends shaping AWS PrivateLink's trajectory rapidly evolve. Advances in PrivateLink technology, driven by strong investment and development, promise to further streamline network architecture, enhance security, and simplify cross-resource accessibility—all creating a robust ecosystem for secure, efficient, and compartmentalized service endpoints.

15.1. Emerging Technologies Impacting AWS PrivateLink

Several emerging technologies are poised to influence AWS PrivateLink's future direction. These technologies, already showing revolutionary potential, will undoubtedly imbue PrivateLink with novel capabilities and optimizations.

Machine Learning and AI stand tall among these technologies. As AWS continues to robustly integrate AI and ML into its services, it's expected that AWS PrivateLink will likewise incorporate these capabilities. AI and ML could facilitate predictive analytics for PrivateLink activities. This feature could proactively identify potential issues and optimize network configurations to reduce latency or improve bandwidth. Moreover, AI-driven automation might further streamline PrivateLink, helping businesses more efficiently utilize resources without manual intervention.

Internet of Things (IoT) will also impact AWS PrivateLink's future. As IoT devices proliferate, networks become more crowded and complex. AWS PrivateLink can simplify this complexity by providing secure, direct connections to microservices and eliminating exposure on public networks.

Blockchain is another technology that redirects the trajectory of PrivateLink. With its decentralized nature, blockchain offers unique challenges in managing endpoints and ensuring secure, reliable connections. AWS PrivateLink could become a key facilitator in securely accessing blockchain services, providing a secure, efficient route to these decentralized resources.

15.2. Security Enhancements

Given the ever-growing threat landscape, it's evident that AWS PrivateLink's development will continue to prioritize security. Increasingly sophisticated cyber threats continually challenge network administrators to protect sensitive business data and keep systems running smoothly.

Advanced security features, including AI-enhanced threat detection and remediation, could be integrated into AWS PrivateLink. Such enhancements might allow quicker response to potential threats, minimizing damage and ensuring service continuity.

Better encryption protocols are also likely to be a focal point, ensuring that data remains secure during transit. Additional security measures, such as multi-factor authentication, might be implemented at the VPC endpoint level to further secure access.

15.3. Increased Global Availability

Currently, AWS PrivateLink is available in various regions globally. However, AWS continuously invests in expanding its global infrastructure, suggesting that PrivateLink's availability will extend even further, serving more locations worldwide. This expansion ensures organizations can access PrivateLink services wherever their business infrastructure resides, reducing latency and improving service efficiency.

15.4. Offering More Native AWS Services

Presently, PrivateLink supports several native AWS services like Amazon EC2, S3, and RDS, among others. Leveraging AWS PrivateLink for these services has shown significant improvements in security and performance when accessing resources. Consequently, we can expect AWS to increase the number of native services supported by PrivateLink, making it a more integral part of AWS architecture.

AWS is also likely to further streamline and enhance the integration between PrivateLink and other native AWS services. Deeper integration promises to provide optimized paths between services, reducing latency and ensuring high availability.

15.5. Greater Support for Third-Party Services

AWS PrivateLink provides secure access to critical third-party SaaS applications without exposing traffic to the public internet. As more businesses migrate essential operations to cloud-based SaaS applications, we can predict AWS will bolster PrivateLink's third-party service support.

This support should not just extend to a greater number of SaaS applications but also aim to strengthen the security and performance of these links. Enhanced partnerships between AWS and SaaS providers could yield optimized and safer connections to essential applications, benefitting both the service providers and their consumers.

Predicting the future of AWS PrivateLink involves analyzing trends in broader technology and cyber-security landscapes alongside AWS's innovation and investment strategies. It's clear that as businesses continue to leverage cloud-based resources, AWS PrivateLink's significance will only expand, continually adapting to the fluctuating needs of digital connectivity and security. While it's difficult to pin down exact future updates and trends, the directional guides discussed above present a strong forecast of what's to come. As such, mastering the current intricacies of troubleshooting AWS PrivateLink will be an invaluable skill in navigating the future IT landscape.